ONE MORE MILE

TESTED BY SUFFERING, CARRIED BY LOVE

ELIZABETH MORGAN

◆ FriesenPress

Suite 300 - 990 Fort St
Victoria, BC, V8V 3K2
Canada

www.friesenpress.com

Copyright © 2021 by Elizabeth Morgan
First Edition — 2021

Thanks to Alexander Grabchilev at Stocksy United Photography for his appealing front cover photo for One More Mile.

Thank you to Megan Edelman Photography for the author photo on back cover.

ISBN
978-1-5255-9830-2 (Hardcover)
978-1-5255-9829-6 (Paperback)
978-1-5255-9831-9 (eBook)

1. *Biography & Autobiography, Religious*

Distributed to the trade by The Ingram Book Company

Disclaimer:

To protect the privacy of family, friends, and doctors, their names have been changed unless they are deceased or have given permission to be named.

DEDICATION

For all who are hurting, who wonder how you will make it through another day:

There's hope for the hopeless. Help is closer than you think.

~

May the God of hope fill you with all joy, and peace, as you trust in him, so that you may overflow with hope by the power of the Holy Spirit.

Romans 15:13—New International Version

TABLE OF CONTENTS

PART 1

CHAPTER 1

A Box of Journals

I very nearly did not give myself a chance to write this story or any other.

My body was fighting end-stage kidney failure, and I likely did not have much time left due to my frailty. Maybe a year, the doctor had told Ron. Thirty-seven was too young to be critically ill and facing my end.

On a crisp fall day, I rolled out our rusty barrel—used for burning garbage—into a clearing in the backyard. Our little boys were at school, and Ron was at work. No one was around to question my plan. Back into the house I went, then dragged out several boxes of steno pads filled with my endless storytelling. In my apron, I carried a wooden box of matches. Enough of this dream of writing a book someday, despite all the well-meaning people who had encouraged that vision. I tossed a wad of newsprint into the barrel, and I reached for a match . . .

Storytelling and writing had played an influential role in my Mennonite heritage. In my grandfather's farm kitchen, Sunday guests sat in a circle after dinner, treating each other to their personal stories—mostly true, but not necessarily—while chewing on toasted sunflower seeds and spitting their shells onto the floor. Later, the aunties swept up the oily bits, leaving a sheen on the hardwood floor. The bonding of storytelling also left a happy glow after the guests departed in their horses and buggies or Model Ts.

When my father's new trucking job took our family east, Dad could get quite long-winded, entertaining our family and friends with his hair-raising trucking adventures. Mom also carried on this tradition, writing about her carefree childhood and the predicaments of motherhood in the form of poetry and short stories—both tender and hilarious. It seemed natural that I too was drawn to stories.

When I was eleven, Mom gave me a moss green diary for Christmas. This gift gave me a safe way to express my private musings. It had a lock and key to assure me that no one would invade my sacred space, especially my rascally five brothers. My sister, with whom I shared a bedroom, was more inclined to respect another's privacy. Yet, what a laughably flimsy security system for a vulnerable adolescent, but I needed to dump my escalating mood swings somewhere.

Journalling provided me with a satisfying vehicle for exploring my doubts, my faith in God, and the lessons learned through suffering. It gave me an avenue for creativity and for sowing seeds of hope in others. No one could predict how invaluable these efforts would prove when life turned very difficult in my thirties, and kidney failure threatened my survival.

Eventually, I bought plain stenographer pads that I filled with urgent prayers to God for relief and solutions. But embedded in the prayers were the vignettes of my young life, which might provide a rich source of material for a book someday.

The book idea came from my mother, my father, and my husband. Each one cheered me on at different times of my life. Mom predicted that someday I would become "a teacher and then a writer." In my mid-thirties, I confided to my father that my journals were taking up too much space. He urged me to keep on recording. I protested that they held sensitive material that should never be published until all parties had passed.

"You never know," Dad said, "if you don't write that book, maybe one of your sons or your future grandchildren will carry on your story."

After moving to Moose Jaw, Saskatchewan, with Ron and our two young sons, I regretted the pressure of too many journals cluttering our storage, my mind, and my time. According to my nephrologist, my precious time was running out at an alarming pace. I crumpled more newsprint and threw it into the barrel for fire starter.

Finally, I struck the match, inhaled its sulphurous odour, and tossed it into the drum. I peered in to ensure the paper was burning. With both hands, I scooped up some of my precious journals and looked into the fire again. Hungry fingers of flame reached upward for more fuel.

What was I thinking? These scribbles represented painful episodes in my journey. But they also held poignant moments of light and hope. *Maybe someone will be helped by your experiences*, Dad had whispered inside my head. I could not do it.

Smothering the flames with a lid, I carried my cargo back into the house.

When Ron came home, I told him what I had nearly done. He expressed relief. "Hon, please promise me you will *never* try that again." He added, "I want you to carry on writing; it is your therapy and your future. You have a gift that should not be wasted." He assured me that we would always make room for my boxes of writing.

My husband is a realist. He knew my time could be short, but he also encouraged our family to make the most of the days we were given. *Now is the time to be happy,* was a motto he embraced and still does.

My parents' and husband's vision for me was confirmed by a surprising fourth source.

CHAPTER 2

A Calling

When I was first hospitalized in the University of Saskatchewan Hospital in 1982 with end-stage renal failure, my social worker, Jacquie Lambie, noticed that I kept a daily journal. "What do you write about?" she probed.

I told her I was dumping my fear and anger onto paper, asking God why a young woman of thirty-seven must suffer a life-threatening condition.

Jacquie wanted to see for herself. I refused. She coaxed me until I surrendered. As she read my entries, which bled rage and terror, Jacquie's red head bobbed, and her pendulum earrings danced with every bob.

"You must write a book about this," she said, tapping her manicured red nails on my journal.

I'm a dying woman, but she thinks I should spend my last months labouring over a book.

"Do you know how many people in this heart and kidney ward feel just like you do?" she asked.

No, I had no idea. I was preoccupied with my own war.

Jacquie explained, "They can't articulate their journey. You must do it for them."

Ron agreed. "This is a calling from God. He gave you the gift to write from the heart. He will give you the time and energy to fulfill it."

In the years that followed, my health took detours between near-death and merciful recovery. Happily, I outlived my doctor's professional prediction. Meanwhile, my confidence in writing a book flipped and flopped. But underneath the doubts, there ran a river of hope in God, who would be my inspiration.

Applying the biblical story of the boy who surrendered his small lunch of a few fish and loaves for Jesus to feed the four thousand, God gave me a picture of how he would use my raw stories to feed many hungry souls. This vision gave me momentum.

My writing courses warned that the trickiest part of writing a memoir is the middle, where the story can drag and lose its focus. I knew that to be true. When my story reached Moose Jaw, Saskatchewan, I hit a roadblock. It was a terrifying time of reliving the reality of my frail condition. Though I was writing this segment long after we had lived through it and had moved to Edmonton, Alberta, I wondered how much more pain could I bear to dredge from this ditch of memories? I kept on stalling.

It took another health crisis to turn me around.

CHAPTER 3

Surviving Listeria

After five trips to the University of Alberta Hospital Emergency in August 2008, I was finally diagnosed with listeria infection—a foodborne, bacterial illness that can be very serious for people older than sixty-five and those with weakened immune systems.

I had read about many deaths from listeria that July, due to contaminated machines in the Maple Leaf food processing plant in Toronto. It never occurred to me that I was vulnerable, since I rarely ate processed meat or cheese. It was the antirejection meds that I was taking to protect my kidney transplant of 1996 along with a nasty case of C. difficile, picked up during a one-night stay in the hospital, that set me up for such a violent hit.

"We are going to try to pull you through," said the infectious disease doctor who delivered the sobering news.

After she left my isolated cubicle in the ER, I felt incredibly calm. "Well, Lord," I whispered to that Living Presence in the room with me, "I guess I'm done here." I was okay with that. It had been a long haul; I was ready to be called Home to God. My shrinking body craved rest.

An aide brought me a full meal, which seemed incongruent with how severely ill I had been a few hours earlier. And yet, I dug in because I was unaccountably hungry. While I relished every bite of mashed potatoes and chicken, feeling completely at peace, I heard a question in my head. *What about the book you started writing a few decades ago?*

Oh, you have got to be kidding! My book is stuck in Moose Jaw, and I'm too tired to move forward.

No answer came back.

It took a month to revive my system and return me to the land of survivors. What also survived was that nagging internal question. *What about the book?*

I knew what I had to do and at least one reason why my life had been spared. My thoughts were consumed with the task at hand. I wrote a promise to myself and to God: *With God's help, I will finish this book.*

Nearly every day, I pulled out my plans and spread them before the Lord, the way King Hezekiah of Judah laid a threatening letter from his enemy before the Lord. And like him, I prayed for direction and reassurance.

How I Got Out of Moose Jaw became my tongue-in-cheek working title and goal. The book, which emerged five years later, was the product of God's Spirit guiding me. God, my chief Author and Finisher, had brought alongside many gifted people to assist me in the process of edits, proofreading, cover and interior design, and publication. Plus, God gave me the title—*Sunny Side of a Rainy Life.*

CHAPTER 4

Labour of Love

While wintering in Victoria, I completed the fine-tuning of my manuscript. It had been a tedious process of rewrites and proofreading, until Ron urged me to release the book to FriesenPress for publication. There will always be errors and second-guessing, he reminded me. "Let it go."

It was a crisp day in early February 2013 when UPS called. They were coming up to my apartment with a delivery order from FriesenPress. I held my breath. This was The Day that I had worked toward for three decades.

While I waited for the UPS driver's arrival at our fifteenth floor, I recorded my response on Photo Booth. The slender brunette of sixty-six, framed in the video, carried the demeanour of a girl who was clapping her hands on Christmas morning. She was jumping out of her skin with repressed joy.

Don't get too excited. This book could be a bust. But I knew it wasn't. I'd poured my heart into this labour of love.

When the UPS driver entered my front hallway, it was apparent he could not have cared less what the box held. *Whatever, ma'am,* his expression seemed to say. "Where do you want 'em?" He dropped the heavy carton on our kitchen table. *Thud!* He could not be expected to know what precious cargo he had just delivered. But God and I knew.

It took a while to slice through the packing tape and open the flaps. There they were.

Fifty glossy 6- x 9-inch books with black lettering.

Sunny Side of a Rainy Life.

ELIZABETH MORGAN in bold letters across the bottom.

In the middle, an italicized quote: *How would our marriage withstand this severe test?* The background was grey with raindrops covering a cheerful yellow umbrella.

Simple and inviting, thanks to my cover designer, Ian West.

Next, I flipped the copy to see the back cover, which summarized the book contents.

> *I thought it was a cruel joke when I was finally diagnosed with a life-threatening disease. . . . No doctor would take me seriously until one day I was told I had late-stage kidney disease, which meant either a lifetime of dialysis—hooked up to a machine—or a kidney transplant. How did I pull it together as a young wife and mother, knowing my life could be tragically short?*
>
> *Finding the sunny side of my rainy life has been a long process. Yet with the support of my husband, children, and friends, I found a renewed purpose*

*in life and a realization of the power and glory
of God.*

The bottom right corner held a black-and-white photo of
the author with her writing credits.

I looked at that younger woman, wearing a white shirt and
jeans. The picture had been taken at a time when my book
seemed close to publication. But because of numerous setbacks
in health, it had taken ten more years to arrive at this pivotal
moment. My cover designer and Ron urged me to stick with
the original photo because it reflected how I looked when most
of the book was written. Besides, it was a perfect author pose
for a cover, they said.

I reluctantly agreed, but I no longer looked like her. Never
mind, the story happened to that *younger* wife and mother.

When Ron arrived home, we shared the thrill of leafing
through the pages, appreciating the interior layout, pausing
over the family photos that traced our journey through the
years of hardship and recovery.

The following day, an emotional tug of war had me wonder-
ing whether I was enjoying this accomplishment too much. A
dear friend, Karen, in Australia wrote me some good advice:
Savour the moment. This selfless giver was giving me permission
to enjoy the fruit of my labours.

Of course, many had assisted me in this process, but in
the end, I had to show up and do the work; do the trusting,
and release the results to my God, who promised to feed the
hungry with my few fish and loaves.

Eight years later, my greatest supporter continues to be my
husband, who shamelessly promotes my book wherever he
goes. We have sold about seven hundred copies through book

talks, book fairs, book signings, and word of mouth, but the rest Ron has given as gifts to people who are looking for an inspiring read.

Completely satisfied with finishing that long project, I thought my writing days were over. During this eight-year break, I had no desire to write another book. But God doesn't stop writing our story.

PART 2

CHAPTER 5

Digging in Again

This leads me to my next project: a sequel memoir. Why another book? Though I have had no desire to write again, I impulsively began a file named Book 2, *just in case there's another book in me.* Ron and I have received numerous requests for more storytelling. People ask, "What comes next? What else have you learned from suffering? Why do you still believe in God?"

It seems the time has arrived to dig in again, to see what transpires. The advantages of living longer than expected—I'm in my seventies now—make a long list, but with them come the difficulties of accepting that I've arrived at the winter of my life.

Winter is my least favourite season. Born near Winnipeg in the cold month of February, I have always held an aversion to the bleakness of winter months. My spirit tends to hibernate.

Mom used to dress me in warm plaids and throw me into a snowdrift with my brothers. While they built snow forts and tunnelled through them, I stood at the door, wailing to be let indoors where I could thaw out.

Here I am in my senior years, still wailing to be let indoors—to a healthier, younger version of myself—but there is no escape from the winter of life. Good thing, too, because I hear that the best wine is made by the aging process.

Often, I ask what God hopes to accomplish by allowing a new season of physical pain or another challenge to my emotional maturity. His answers are making ripples and, sometimes, titanic waves on our horizon.

CHAPTER 6

God's Waves and Billows

It was a memorable event in the spring of 2016 that floored my husband and me.

I didn't know when I headed out to meet Ron for our weekly date that I would end up in a diaper by the end of the day.

It was a sun-warmed May morning. My husband had just returned from delivering our belongings in a U-Haul to our future home in Victoria. We planned to drive there in three weeks, once the sale of our Edmonton condo was completed.

We decided to meet for our usual Friday hot dog and banana split sundae date at Southgate Mall. Ron cycled there, while I took the LRT, Edmonton's light rail train. This rendezvous was one that we always enjoyed, but this one was especially meaningful because it was likely our last date before moving to the West Coast.

As my train approached the station, I texted Ron my usual heads-up, "I am only five minutes away." Feeling in especially high spirits, I added an emoticon of a person *running* plus a puff of wind to indicate *speed*—the joke being that I have not been able to run in decades.

After deboarding, I took the elevator up to the causeway leading to the mall, using my trusty cane to stabilize me. But as my elevator reached the second floor, I noticed a commotion involving the LRT police and a crowd directly in front of the exit. I considered how to safely navigate around this potentially troublesome gathering. The group of people had their backs to me, so I skirted behind them to the right.

Things can happen with lightning speed, like my emoticons had suggested. Except, I was not going to arrive at our date today.

As I passed behind one large, young man, he suddenly stepped backward and directly into me, striking me with his bulging backpack.

I can still see it in my head. The way my body turned in the air, my cane flying out of reach, my right side slamming onto the floor, my forehead crashing onto concrete, and then rolling onto my back. Wild-eyed, I lay stunned, but conscious.

Someone ran to me. "Are you okay?"

"NO!" I yelled.

Men in blue uniforms circled me. Someone knelt next to me.

Questions . . . a lot of questions.

"Can you move? Can you get back up? Who can we call?"

"Ron Morgan." I even remembered his cell number, which is not always the case. "Oh," I added, "he's in the mall. Only five minutes away."

Poor Ron! Only five minutes away. But I would never get there. He would be so alarmed.

Nausea billowed in my throat. And curiously, I started to yawn.

A young police officer talked quietly to me, asked more questions, encouraged me to deep breathe and stay awake. I had an overwhelming desire to sleep.

When Ron arrived, the officer explained what had happened and said an ambulance was on its way. Normally, I object to anything so dramatic or costly as an ambulance, but this time, I knew I needed to cooperate.

My head felt like it was smashed in. Did I have a concussion? A brain bleed? Was this the end of me?

I think this will be the end of me.

Just when we had made the big decision to permanently leave Edmonton, Alberta, and its premier health-care system, which had maintained my kidney transplant of twenty years and my previous life on hemodialysis for thirteen years. After my transplant from my brother, Dave, we had bought a condo in Victoria—our compact cottage in the sky—where I could safely winter without the risk of falling and breaking my fragile bones. Now, we were planning to make the permanent move to Victoria.

We had taken this step in faith that God would provide us with good health support in British Columbia, though my kidney doctor warned me it would take years to find a kidney match, should I need another one. My transplanted kidney function had been hovering in the low twenties for some years. Although it allowed me a pretty good life, it reacted to every flu bug, minor surgery, or injury by dropping into the teens.

When Ron saw me lying on the floor, his first concern was my kidney transplant. It was tucked into the right side of my abdomen, the side I had fallen on.

Surprisingly, I never gave my kidney a thought. My primary concern was how devastating it would be for Ron to see me lying motionless on the floor. Another crisis with my health. Another thing to navigate. Another thing for us to overcome.

By the time Ron arrived, he had managed to access the compartment in his brain called *logic*.

The young officer was prepared to talk down the distraught husband—except Ron was rational as usual, ready to gauge the damage and to consider how to resolve it.

Everyone around me was calm and reassuring. Ambulance attendants took over, lifting me onto a stretcher and driving me to the hospital of my choice—the University of Alberta Hospital, where my kidney specialist had her practice.

Ron followed behind on his bicycle, asking God why he had allowed this accident to happen at this time in our lives, just when we were in the midst of a move to another province, and why to Liz who had seen so many medical trials. Could God not have protected her fragile frame from this fall? Ron had believed his daily prayers would keep his bride safe.

As for me, I was too numb to ask any angry questions of God, not yet. Not that I could spell out.

CHAPTER 7

Five Feet Away

As I review this month-long story from the vantage point of recovery, I have already forgotten most of the awful moments and many of the wonderful ones, that gave me glimpses of what God was up to in allowing this mishap.

So, what do I do with this story, this fading memory? It's not one that I enjoy reviewing. It was a time of misery and terror; yet it had a positive impact on me in the long-run.

I think I am a different person. I think I have changed my view of God a bit, have grown stronger through this trial. I think I am more grateful, calmer, more ready to embrace life with its risks, to take risks, step up to the plate, and live more fully until it is time to go. I think I was being trained in spiritual warfare with every day that passed in the hospital.

Though, it seemed like a relatively brief lesson, it had the potential to end badly.

This was not the first hospital experience that would initially leave me demoralized. But this time, it looked impossible for me to move through the excruciating pain. If I didn't cooperate and try to get out of bed, I would become an invalid.

What was God trying to do to me? I was more frightened than angry. I felt trapped in my body of horrific pain. Not only had I sustained a severe concussion, it took several tests to discover a fractured hip.

Thankfully, a daily dose of hydromorphone became my friend, allowing me to endure being turned for diaper changes. But it yielded other benefits. When friends came to visit, they commented that I was very cheerful for a person in pain. Ron confirmed that was the case. I hadn't noticed. He was adamant that I not get used to the high the narcotic gave me. "You've got to be prepared to cut back your doses." My husband became a nag about this point. He knew that drug addiction could produce its own nightmare.

Around day three, Ron asked if I had looked at myself in a mirror yet.

"No, I don't have a mirror, and I really don't care."

He suggested that I take a selfie on my cellphone. After his visit, I decide to survey the damage.

The woman I saw was not the well-groomed picture of health that I had seen when I embarked on our date, a few days earlier. Besides the dishevelled hair, my eyes were ringed black, like a raccoon's, with significant purple bruising, from my head slamming into the cement. No wonder my head throbbed.

Instead of crying with dismay, I laughed at how scary I looked; spontaneously, I sent the photo that I had taken to my *Facebook* page. Morphine was definitely responsible for my response.

After a brief nap, I returned to *Facebook* to cancel my post. Too late! Eight people had already sent their condolences, with promises of prayer support. Thereafter, more messages poured in to reassure me that I was not alone. I'm a reluctant *Facebook* user because of privacy issues, plus the gobbling up of time, but social media gave me a positive experience. I had not realized how much I needed my real and virtual friends at this time

Day by day, I began to see God at work in my crisis. He sent daily markers of his presence through the ongoing prayers of many cheerleaders—visitors, caregivers, doctors, and Internet friends—who came to run with me to the finishing line.

He sent laughter, in the midst of humiliating diaper changes. Most of my caregivers were Filipino women, who served with cheerful demeanours, often giggling and talking about trivia as they turned me over each time. No big deal for them to provide this unpleasant, but necessary care.

Though he detests the hospital environment, Ron came each day to support me. In my teens and early twenties, I was a hospital ward aide, so for me, hospitals are not as intimidating as they could be. But for him, visiting was a determined effort, especially when it became clear I was not thriving.

At the end of each day, my faithful husband held my hand, praying for God's care over me. Ron is known as a man of his word and a man of prayer. How blessed I am to be on his team.

Ron even stayed with me and held me steady when I had to disimpact myself. I had to perform this procedure because the nighttime nursing staff had no authority to perform this humiliating task for me without a doctor's approval.

Lying in bed all day, pumped full of narcotics, created an impossible situation for all patients' colons on the broken hip ward. Mine was made worse by a historically lazy colon and irritable bowel syndrome. Nausea and pressure rippled through my abdomen.

The nurses provided me with lubrication and gloves, but they were only authorized to stand by. With a disgusted sigh, I proceeded to take on the task while they observed my humiliation. Ron stood by as well to emotionally support me and steady my trembling knees. After about a half hour, I finally achieved success, dropping back on my pillow with exhaustion.

After my nurses cleaned me up, straightened my covers, and pulled the curtains back, they left Ron and me to our privacy. When they left, I wondered if this is how we felt as babies, after our mothers changed and powdered us down. *Ah, dry and comfortable again.* After these thoughts, finally, I dared to look over at Ron. He wore a little smile.

"What?" I asked.

He whispered, "I was pushing so hard with you that I nearly had a bowel movement too."

Oh, the giggles. We laughed and laughed at our predicament. No doubt, others were amused as well. It wasn't that different from trying to push out a baby, except the consequences of the latter last a lifetime.

When my roommate's family passed our open curtain on their way out, they waved to us, commenting on how glad they were that I had finally gotten relief.

Oh, no! They too, had witnessed the moans, the odour; the most embarrassing moment of my life. But I suppose they had already seen it all with their own mom suffering dementia. It's all a matter of perspective, isn't it?

But after that experience, I fantasized about being able to reach the washroom at the end of my bed. Five feet, but it looked like five miles. Somehow, God would get me there.

CHAPTER 8

Roommates

Meanwhile, my roommate, Elsa, distracted me with her indomitable spirit.

Though she howled in agony each time she was taken to the bathroom, she could walk with ease when the pain meds took effect. It seemed her dementia allowed her to completely forget that she had a serious fracture. Every few hours, I saw her feet flop over the side of her bed, preparing to land on the floor.

"Elsa! Get back in bed!" I urged her. "Call the nurse to help you before you hurt yourself."

She learned to listen to my voice, but she tried this stunt many times a day and through the night too. I was exhausted, watching her, but I couldn't bear for her to suffer a worse injury. We were all suffering with immense pain. Echoes down the hallway of fellow patients howling in the night, especially those with dementia, disturbed all our sleep and nerves.

One evening, when I was finally able to sit beside my bed for an hour and was reading a little devotional called "God on the Throne," a soft German voice startled me.

"Elsa, what are you doing?"

"I have come to visit you," she said softly and proceeded to sit in the chair beside me.

It was too late to send her back to her bed, so we chatted for a while. Elsa said she wished she could go home and work in her garden. Her children had told me their mother was a sturdy gardener.

Elsa posed an interesting question. "I wonder where I will go after this?"

"Do you mean after you leave the hospital?"

"No . . . when I die."

As I pondered the best way to answer, my friend abruptly got up and walked back to her bed unaided, just as she had come.

Please, Lord, give me a chance to respond. He did.

About fifteen minutes later, Elsa returned. This time she sat on the edge of my bed, and then with a coy expression, she rolled on her side and slid under my covers, smiling at me.

"Elsa," I asked, "do you like *my* bed?" Perhaps, she was confused, thinking it was her bed?

"Yah."

After a while, I asked, "Elsa, do you plan to spend the night with me?"

"Yah." Big grin.

Here was my open door. "Elsa, earlier you asked me where you will go when you die? Can I tell you what Jesus said about that?"

She nodded. I explained.

On the night that Jesus was arrested and going to die on a cross, he told his disciples that he was going away. They wanted to know where he was going. He explained he was preparing a place for them, that where he is, they may be also. They protested that they did not know the way. But Jesus clearly said, "I am the way . . . no man comes to the Father but by me."

"So, Elsa, if we believe that Jesus is the way to Heaven and depend on him, he will take us safely Home as well."

I paused. Was any of this making sense? How to connect this message with my friend who was in various stages of alertness?

"Elsa, I see that you are a good woman, and so am I. But none of our good works will carry us far enough. Only what Jesus did for us on the cross, dying for us, will carry us all the way Home.

"Elsa, do you know about Jesus?"

"Yah."

"Have you ever decided to put your trust in him and not in yourself?"

She wasn't sure.

"Well, you can do that anytime, and he will hear you."

She nodded. After a few minutes, my interloper rolled out of bed. "I think I will go back to *my own* bed."

Aha! So, she did know this was not her bed. We both laughed as I got back in my bed, already warmed for me.

Around midnight, I awoke to find Elsa, bed and all, being wheeled out of our room. Apparently, she had wandered off the ward as soon as I had drifted asleep. Nursing staff parked her bed close to their station after that incident.

Before we parted company, I was thrilled to be given a chance to bring my neighbour the good news story of our destination as God's children. Jesus is always the way—the way and the truth.

Another elderly woman arrived on a stretcher, also with dementia, whose concerned daughter visited every day. The mom was proving to be hard to please. One day, her daughter said, "Mama, you were unhappy in x; you were unhappy at y; you are unhappy here. I don't think you will be happy even with Heaven."

I stifled a laugh and said I was sure she would be happy in Heaven.

Her daughter announced, "I have been to Heaven."

A few days later, I asked her about that. When she had undergone critical cancer surgery six years earlier, she had left the table and gone to Heaven for a time. She said she met God, who had curly hair with purple highlights.

Purple hair, hmmm . . . the colour of royalty. I grinned to myself. I wondered how reliable her story was. But she sounded convincing. She said that God told her she had to come back.

She had protested, "Why does it have to hurt so much to die?" She didn't want to return to life and then die again.

God had answered her, "It is for my Son."

At that moment, I began to weep. For his Son. That resonated for me. I did not know what God meant exactly, but it touched me.

Maybe, I was here, suffering this indignity and excruciating moments of pain, for his Son as well. He had a reason for allowing this, and I was searching to justify my presence in these wards, aside from the obvious reason of my fracture.

Was it to bloom in this place? To proclaim Jesus as my Lord? To be a testimony to the Living Presence of the Lord in my life, and to give that same hope to my fellow travellers?

One charge nurse, who was changing my new roommate's bed, pondered aloud why a relatively young woman of sixty-nine like me had been sent to this fracture ward, which usually housed only patients in their eighties and nineties, many with dementia. My nurse alluded to a deeper meaning than the obvious fracture.

She referred to an incident report earlier in the week, when I had witnessed another nurse carelessly toss Elsa's legs back into bed, as she tried to get up without help.

My nurse suggested it was so I could witness, report the abuse, and stand up to it on Elsa's behalf. My nurse said she had been trying to get this nurse disciplined for her rough bedside manner. Now, it had been officially addressed, so that she would be more aware and accountable.

It was gratifying to think God might have planted me there to protect Elsa and, potentially, others.

But I did not appreciate being the recipient of another lesson in my life of chronic illness. Pain terrified me. It took many cheerleaders to motivate me to begin the process of moving my body through the pain, of learning how to roll out of bed, stand up, and walk again.

Bahrain, a lead nurse, was among those who tried to coax me to start moving out of bed. He had come to give me numerous pep talks. These attempts annoyed me because he seemed stern and patronizing. He was insistent that I try harder.

One morning, however, he disarmed me by meeting me at gut level. He brought my chart with him, explaining that he had read it from start to finish. It had given him a clear picture of my medical journey, since my early years of dialysis. He laid out my history, naming each setback. "You survived that, and you survived that too." He made it clear that I had come through remarkable challenges. Until, that is, he arrived at my current pelvic fracture, which was immobilizing me through terrible pain.

He said, "You can survive this, too—but only *one* person can decide that. You!"

I was greatly touched that Bahrain had taken the time to read my whole chart and to give me another pep talk. Who cares that much? Only GOD. He's the one who sent this messenger of hope.

I could hear Jesus calling me, as he did his disciples, "If anyone wishes to come after Me, he must deny himself, take up his cross and follow Me." Luke 9:23

Four days later, four friends all showed up at once, not knowing they would witness my first efforts to get out of bed. As my physical therapist coached me through the mechanics, my friends held their collective breath and, literally, prayed me up on my feet. God infused me with palpable strength as I rolled over to sit up that first time and then to stand up. Eventually, a few days later, I took those early agonizing steps to the bathroom—only five feet away.

Bob Logue, our totally blind friend, who brought giant cookies from Starbucks for Ron and me to share, was one of those witnesses to the breathing presence of the Holy Spirit during that maiden voyage from my bed to a standing position. Bob told me later that he could not see with his eyes, but he could sense the supernatural outpouring of God's power.

Of course, Ron was my ultimate support. How he touched my spirit when he held my hand at the end of each day, humbly bowing his head to commit my care and rest for another night in the hospital to the Father.

Taking up our cross seems to be an ongoing call from God, but I'm learning to trust there is purpose in all he asks and all that he allows to come our way. It's a lifelong process.

CHAPTER 9

Alone with God

Sometimes, God removes the myriad of cheerleaders from our circumstances, so we can lean more into him. This was the case two years later, after we had settled into life in Paradise, otherwise known as Victoria, British Columbia.

After my husband, Ron, dropped me off at the Jubilee Hospital in Victoria, I waited my turn to be processed through the assembly line for surgery. A surgery I dreaded because it meant the end of a dialysis-free era and a return to an old one of dialysis dependence, three times a week.

Friends offered to sit with me until I was called, but I sensed a need to be alone. After decades of enduring my chronic kidney illness with me, no one knew that better than my spouse. Ron understood that I needed room to breathe, to listen for God's still voice of comfort without the distraction of well-meaning people.

While I waited my turn, my thoughts were preoccupied with my brother, Dave, in Ontario. Twenty-two years earlier, he had given me his kidney. Now, it was quickly failing. How generously and willingly he had offered this gift to rescue me from thirteen years of hemodialysis and, more importantly, to keep me alive. But our transplanted kidney was limping to the finish line. It was February 27, 2018.

Two weeks earlier, Dave had assured me, through faint whispers, that my kidney would recover. He was praying fervently, trusting God to do a miracle. He even offered me his other kidney, since he was dying, but doctors said that was not going to happen. He had pancreatic cancer; therefore, there was no guarantee that his remaining kidney would be cancer-free.

Watching the wall clock, I thought, *it can't be much longer until my turn.* I recalled a story about Dave, e-mailed to me that morning by our youngest brother, Jim, in Manitoba. I reached for my cellphone. Now, would be a good time to read it.

Despite the sombre atmosphere in the waiting room, I could not help myself. I laughed out loud, reading the details of Dave's inquisitive and determined spirit.

> *As a baby confined to his crib, Davey wanted to know what was going on in the next room. He howled to be noticed. When ignored, he decided to remedy the matter. Jogging his sturdy body back and forth, he forced the crib to jump forward. He managed to jiggle the crib across his bedroom floor, down the hallway, and into the kitchen. "Even his high chair had to be anchored to the kitchen floor with cable and eyebolts to prevent it from catapulting to the ground," Jim wrote.*

This hilarious story was typical of Dave's stubborn will that would not accept *no* or *can't* as an answer. His desire to help others was one of his greatest gifts.

A receptionist interrupted my musings. "Marie Morgan! Please, follow me," she called.

Marie is my legal name. I never thought to ask my parents why they called me by my middle name, Elizabeth. I don't always respond to Marie, but this time I was ready to get this over with.

Shunted from one station to another in an efficient manner, I was finally lying under crisp sheets, waiting for my surgical team to fetch me. Should I mention to someone that I had experienced chest pain in the night? It didn't seem relevant; it had probably been heartburn.

What did seem relevant was the pain in my spirit.

A nurse was taking my vitals one more time. Like the previous nurses, I gave her a piece of information that I hoped would bring a response of comfort. Pointing to my abdomen where my transplanted kidney was located, I said to my caregiver, "My brother, Dave, who gave me this kidney, died last week. Today he is being *buried*."

Nothing.

Each nurse had a job to do and a timeline to fill. Patients needed to be fully processed and ready when their surgical team came to roll them into surgery. But nothing? It was almost as if none of them could hear my plea for empathy. Had my words become inaudible to them?

Hadn't I sensed that I needed to be *alone* with God today? He was the One with ultimate words of comfort for my soul. He would provide the tenderness I needed, when I needed it.

"Okay, Mrs. Morgan, sorry we're late. It's your turn." My team whisked me away.

Once more, we discussed the nature of the surgery, which was to rebuild a new fistula in my left arm—to prepare for hemodialysis. Again.

My surgeon asked me how they could make me more comfortable, given the severe pain of arthritis in both of my shoulders. Gently, the team took time to manipulate my body onto the surgical table, until I was in a position of comfort. My tears rolled. Kindness at such a time moved me beyond my grief. God was touching me through their hands and tone.

At the very hour when surgery was beginning, my family in Steinbach was committing Dave's body into the ground near our Dad's, Mom's, and oldest brother, Bill's, graves.

But none of my deceased loved ones were really there. Their spirits had flown to be with the Lord they had served while on earth. The popular song "I'll Fly Away" expresses this joyful hope for God's children.

CHAPTER 10

Comfort from a Stranger

A week after fistula surgery, I again woke in the night at home with chest pain and excessively high blood pressure. By morning, my pressures had increased. I was instructed to proceed to the Emergency where I was quickly given a bed and monitored. This immediate response alarmed me more than my symptoms, which I had convinced myself and Ron were really *nothing*.

Years ago, Ron and I had agreed that I am often better on my own in hospitals since he becomes a tiger where my well-being is concerned. I learned to negotiate my health care in a quiet, firm way—thanks to Ron's able coaching.

However, this event was terrifying for us both. What to do?

Ron told his small prayer and Bible team about my heart dilemma that followed the fistula surgery. One woman jumped up. "I want to go and comfort Elizabeth." Wild horses could not have stopped her.

Ron gave me a heads-up. He was sending a very compassionate woman that he trusted, but I vaguely knew her.

Really, Ron? A stranger?

And yet, not entirely. I knew some of her backstory. Just one look at the right side of her face and you knew she had a war story. Cancer had buried its greedy fingers around her eye, her cheek, her jaw. After removal of the tumours and years of painful reconstruction, she was left with a frozen left side. And an endearing, one-sided smile.

"Hi, Liz. I've come to sit with you for the rest of the day." Michelle's lovely blue eyes looked full of concern.

She propped my pillow, tucked the sheets around me, gave me slow sips of water, and talked. Did I tell you she was a talker? Non-stop.

What good can come from this? I muttered to myself.

God must have been chuckling behind his holy hand since he orchestrates our lives to bring blessings.

As the hours passed, Michelle kept me distracted with her nervous chatter. This was probably the best thing for me, given the serious investigation of my heart. After hearing her story, I could not feel too sorry for myself. This brave warrior had come to comfort me even while her own life was loaded with chaos. I sensed deep compassion in her body language. She reassured me that I was going to be okay, surrounded by prayers and God's love.

Later that day, I was admitted to the heart ward for a week of further testing.

It was weeks after I came home before Michelle surfaced again, but I had not forgotten her kindness to me. We arranged to meet for lunch at Murchie's Tea where she presented me with a set of dainty booklets with stylized birds and flowers on the covers.

"So you can write your prayer requests in pretty notebooks," she said. My heart melted.

This relative *stranger*, who came to my rescue in the ER, had found her way to my guarded heart with her open-hearted, open-handed love. Nothing put on. Just authentic grace. I learned that, besides talking, she is very good at listening with her heart.

Since our ER experience together, we have gone through several more surgeries—hers.

More cosmetic surgery to build up her sunken cheek with cow skin. And then, the startling discovery and removal of seven more tumours. Thankfully, this time they were benign, but brutally invasive. Even her ear had to be removed to get at the tumours and then reattached.

"Perseverance, Liz!" Michelle often reminds us both. "We've got to persevere. God has got this."

CHAPTER 11

Heart Issues

I'm not eager to review my week in the heart ward, but it seems to be a necessary part of my history. I had never experienced heart issues before, though they're a common complaint among kidney patients. I thought I had escaped that bullet.

Here I was, lying in a hospital ward again, waiting for my fistula to mature, so I could be ready for dialysis when my kidney function dropped a few more points. Ron and I were not relishing that prospect.

But more immediately was the matter of heart palpitations that felt like panic attacks. They could last minutes or hours.

When I first arrived on the heart ward, one nurse, who checked my chart, said, "I see your primary care doctor is Dr. H. You have a very smart doctor!" This was reassuring. I heard this more than once.

Nearly every day, my tall, attractive kidney specialist came in, wearing her stiletto heels, power suit, perfect coif, and cheerful smile to oversee my care. She was a busy physician with a practice at the University of British Columbia in Vancouver as well, so I appreciated the extra time she spent to cheer me on.

Our conversations were frank and frightening. I told her I suspected that I was too frail to handle dialysis again, and now, with this heart condition, it looked like double jeopardy. In addition, my doctor had recently seen signs in my blood work of bone cancer, and we were awaiting testing for that. I had already decided that I did not want to submit myself to cancer treatment. It would be too much.

My doctor did not pretend everything was fine. She agreed that dialysis and heart problems and cancer could be too hard on me. Many do face all these challenges at once, she pointed out. But if my body could not adapt, she would support me in refusing treatment. We talked about how a time comes when the system has had enough.

I asked what to do in the event of a possible heart attack. How would they revive me? Dr. H described how the heart is pounded to restart it. We both looked at my slender frame. My bones were fragile at best and would break like twigs on impact. Not something I would want to survive, it was agreed.

I could sign a do-not-resuscitate order.

For me, this option was a relief. But for Ron, this was unthinkable. And yet, he knew I needed to make the call.

I had already decided.

I cannot begin to describe the grief of this moment between us. The shock and dismay. The unspoken messages . . . after a long, courageous battle, was I willing to give up? How could

I agree to surrender without another fight? It was too soon to give up.

The week ended more hopefully than it had begun. I did not have bone cancer! I did not have a heart attack. My symptoms were caused by Atrial Fibrillation, which I could learn to live with. Now, however, I was more prone to stroke than heart attack.

Though I faced the prospect of dialysis, it could be delayed until the numbers dropped a few more points.

For several months after my discharge, I experienced more alarming heart disturbances—chest pains, weakness, shallow breathing—that took me to the Emergency a few times. An OR doctor and A-Fib clinician urged patients to learn how to tolerate the disturbances by waiting them out at home for up to twenty-four hours. After a while, I figured out that lying down and breathing deeply through them was a good plan. Learning to relax and stress less about this condition helped the episodes to de-escalate.

Two and half years later, I often forget I have the condition. Furthermore, my kidney function has surprised all of us by creeping upward a few points until it has now reached the upper teens. Not much to survive on, but for me it is enough.

When I was on the heart ward, Dr. H had asked me, "What do you want God to do for you?"

So wonderful to have a doctor who speaks the language of faith with me!

I was embarrassed to admit it, but I told her, "Ron and I are asking God if I could please never need to go back on dialysis again."

My doctor said that she was in agreement and would pray for that as well. We talked about how God is still in the business of miracles.

Is this reprieve our miracle?

Perhaps it is a temporary grace, but we'll take it. It has been unfolding in increments—though at first glance, it did not look like a miracle.

After all that intricate work to construct a new fistula on my left arm, it did not function because I lost blood flow to my fingers, causing deep throbbing pain and numbness. Dialysis would only intensify the pain of this condition, called Steal Syndrome. Furthermore, I risked losing my fingers, which had turned blue.

After many months delay, another surgery was finally arranged. This time the fistula had to be disconnected. My surgeon suggested I stay awake for this surgery to eliminate the stress of anesthetic on my system. Previously, I had chosen to be put to sleep, but I trusted his advice. A nurse held my hand to keep me calm while Dr. Roberts performed his magic behind the green drop cloth. There was such a gentle, reaffirming manner about my young surgeon.

I was surprised that I was able to get through that ordeal with less internal distress than usual—must have been the Holy Spirit delivering his peace through my nerve endings.

"Thou wilt keep him in perfect peace whose mind is stayed on thee." Isaiah 26:3

My new reality is that without a working fistula, the alternative is risky. Should I ever need dialysis again, it will be delivered through a central line into the jugular vein. Not the safest means because infection could bring serious consequences, but it is an option used by many. For the moment, dialysis is not an issue. That is God's business; I'm leaving it with him.

We rejoice that he is at work on our behalf to strengthen our confidence in him, to build our character so that we resemble him a bit more than before each setback.

CHAPTER 12

Adapting to Victoria

Apart from the amazing medical miracle of reaching my early seventies, I faced another kind of challenge: adapting to retirement in Victoria.

Night was falling, and I looked forward to my husband's return from another volunteer stint at the inner-city outreach centre. After Ron had settled in front of the television to unwind, I broached the subject of his newfound interest.

"Ron, I think that Our Place is going to take over our lives," I declared.

During our winter forays to Victoria, Ron had found his niche at Our Place—an outreach centre for the marginalized of Pandora Street. But since our permanent move, his voluntary involvement had escalated.

This dismayed me greatly. Ron did not dispute my comment.

ONE MORE MILE

My husband has never been happier than in retirement, discovering God has gifted him with the ability to connect with street people. Ron had experienced success as a merchandizer and franchise owner of several Home Hardware stores, but this new calling was a welcome surprise. Working with the marginalized is where he feels most at home.

Ron's roots were in working-class Saint John, New Brunswick, where his mom worked as a New Brunswick telephone operator in the fifties, and his dad was a newspaper reporter. Since both parents had to be employed to afford their humble tenement rental, Ronnie, their only child whom they had adopted with much love, would buy his lunch at the corner diner and pharmacy, where the owner kept a watchful eye on him.

Ron became street smart at a young age, savouring his independence. Though Arnie was an alcoholic, Ron never considered his family life as challenging. Mae held the family together with her grit and spirit, while Arnie was a gentle person at heart. Their family of three was quite content with their lot. At the end of every day, the Morgans gathered around their chrome-rimmed kitchen table to share a hearty meal of cabbage with corned beef or Mae's yummy meat loaf and scalloped potatoes. Ron came from humble roots and, like his parents, connected well with those who were down and out.

I was thrilled that Ron had found a meaningful way to spend his retirement years—hadn't we both prayed this outcome for a man who needed to stay relevant and active? Otherwise, he could lose his vibrancy and become reclusive.

But I *felt* trapped and isolated on this island. Where did I fit in when my system needed far more rest than my healthy, energetic husband's? Thank God, he had the resilience and

47

commitment to support me through decades of chronic illness! But I had anticipated more time together, not less.

We still had our Saturday dates, which Ron faithfully held to as he had promised many decades earlier, but I wanted more of him during the week. Was that a realistic expectation?

I read in a number of inspirational articles that a person can place far too much responsibility on another person, especially a spouse, to make them happy. That statement stuck with me. Thankfully, I gradually recognized that I was burdening Ron with an impossible task. He was already an over-the-top husband, trying to meet every need. But he knew when to take care of himself as well. And what he needed was to stay very busy in useful service. I concluded that the responsibility of finding my own place of fulfillment fell to me. I was going to have to figure out how to make the most of my home-alone time.

If you've ever visited or seen photos of Victoria, you will know that it is a stunning place to be *trapped* in, but for now, its beauty wasn't enough.

Looking down from our fifteenth-story apartment window at the ocean and picturesque James Bay Village below, I asked God, "What can I do to make this better? What will satisfy my thirst?"

As I read God's Word each day, the answer became clear.

You can pray more urgently for your husband because he needs spiritual strength for the work he has been given. Without it, he can't do the job well.

Ron revealed that he could sense a heavy spiritual darkness whenever he entered the gateway of Our Place. It would take prayer to sustain him and all others who worked there.

I had already developed the habit of praying for him. But this was different. I was being *called by God* to support Ron in a more focused and deliberate way.

My life in Victoria was taking on a specific direction. Though behind the scenes, my prayer calling was vital to Ron's public ministry. God places us all somewhere to bloom.

Each day began in concentrated prayer for Ron while he left early to meet and greet with the members of Our Place. Recording these prayers in a tiny notebook allowed me to track my requests and how God was answering them.

Throughout the day, God reminded me to lift up prayers to Heaven for Ron's refreshment in the midst of an oppressive environment of unhappy, angry people.

In addition, I was casting about for a Bible study to attend, but the one offered to me in our neighbourhood did not satisfy what I was looking for. I didn't know yet what I was searching for, but I knew I hadn't found it yet.

Meanwhile, Ron's involvement with church and Our Place committees continued to snowball because he was eager to serve the community, and he was gifted in administration. One day, he asked if I would write up the next Bible study that he was leading at Our Place because he was short on time.

This activity filled a need in me to get deeper into God's Word. I enjoyed the exploration. My husband saw that and suggested I do a few more studies for him. It released him to fulfill his other obligations, and this work allowed me another way to encourage my husband.

After Ron had presented each lesson, I enquired, "How did the Bible study go?" I wanted to hear about the people coming and the answers they supplied to my questions, so each lesson could be tailored to their needs. I learned their names and what they wanted a prayer for. My prayer journal was filling with their requests. And yet, I had never met one of them. God had planted a seed of compassion in me for these strangers whose life experiences were foreign to me.

Finally, Ron suggested I come to see for myself. I was reluctant. That was his space, not mine. However, he persuaded me that I should give it a try.

When I first started attending, I was intent upon learning what made this marginalized population tick. The *family members*, as they are called at Our Place, challenged my stereotyping of street people as loafers and complainers. They continually surprised me with their insight, tenderness, courage, and survival skills.

At my first meeting, I quietly entered the roundtable session, looking for an empty chair. When I attempted to sit down, a woman slammed her hand down on the chair.

"NO! This seat is taken!"

Seeing another empty chair on the other side of this lady, I proceeded to sit down. Another hand slam. "NO!"

My face reddened. Someone pulled out another chair for me, which I gladly accepted.

The study was invigorating, but week after week, this baffling charade continued with this woman I'll call Olive. When I asked the Our Place chaplain what might be the cause, she pointed out that Olive probably has an IQ of a twelve-year-old.

Rather than try to figure out why she reacted to me in particular, I made sure I did not further aggravate her by sitting near her. Even at our lunch table in the dining room, this scenario continued. One day, all the chairs were spoken for except the one across from me. Olive seated her large frame with a tentative glance my way. Group conversation turned to the mild earthquake that had occurred in the early hours of that day. While everyone was engaged in discussion about that event, Olive remained quiet. She seemed deep in thought.

I did not expect what followed. Olive looked directly at me and asked, "If something happens, will you look after me?"

"Oh . . . my goodness! Of course, I will," I promised.

Her next question: "Should we all dive under this table if there's another quake?"

I agreed that was a good plan.

Olive stuck her white curly head under the table, popped up, checked all of us out—some larger, some smaller—and then at her own generous girth.

She whispered, "I don't think we can all *fit* under there."

I threw back my head and laughed. Olive joined me. Had we just made a connection?

Weeks later, I spotted Olive on the Pandora sidewalk. I had been absent from Bible study due to a cold. I kept walking past her in case she still wanted to avoid me or had forgotten our positive encounter. Yet instinct nudged me to stop. I paused and turned around. Olive was watching me.

When we made eye contact, she threw open her arms. I gladly went back and received her bear hug. Such a simple gesture, and yet it filled me with joy; Olive and I had built a bridge. I think God was in it.

It had been an eye-opener to discover how much power a childlike mind could hold over a supposedly stable adult. It took me back to my own childhood days on the playground when I was chosen last for teams. Rejection can feel deflating, but it can also motivate a person to rise above and figure out what really matters. I concluded that this experience with Olive could teach me something significant:

It is Jesus who ultimately defines us because his insight and love is constant and never fails us the way we do with one another.

CHAPTER 13

Offering Friendship

The experiences of those who frequented Our Place far surpassed mine in the area of being failed and betrayed by people responsible for their care. It tore me up when I heard their stories of heartbreak.

A common theme was abusive parents and foster parents who had kicked their children to the curb. Without the grounding of a nurturing childhood, how could a person be expected to shake off their sense of worthlessness?

Some had been given good families, but mental illness had created bizarre distortions in their belief system. Many could not recognize that their perspective was tainted by chemical imbalance, driven by anger at a society that continued to reject them, or created by the *black dog* of depression, alcoholism, drugs, and poor choices.

I listened more than I contributed at the first Bible study discussions that I attended. Who was I to speak into lives that I could not identify with?

By trial and error, I learned how to connect on some level because of God's compassion in me for their brokenness. Bonding with *family members* came by slow degrees and helped to build my confidence. To be accepted by a shrewd street person is a high honour. They can see through fake every time.

One shaggy street person, Pierre, loved to share his poetry with anyone willing to listen. I met him in Bible study. It was not difficult to find common ground with him because I too enjoy the written word. Pierre demonstrated a great love for God in his poetry and in the way he could recognize the need in someone else, whether she was poor, like him, or better off.

Ron suggested that I could try being a volunteer in spiritual care for the bustling reception area of Our Place—a place to hang out during the day, where people drop in for a coffee and snack.

On my first shift at the Drop-in Centre, Pierre noticed my reluctance to approach strangers and offer my ear. He sat quietly next to me in the long row of chairs against one wall. After a while, he asked me if he might suggest some keys to reaching out to strangers. In his soft French accent, he whispered, "Let the Holy Spirit guide you with his heart of compassion. You have the capacity to care. That's what people need . . . someone who cares and will listen." Then, he placed a hand on my shoulder and prayed with me for courage. Pierre was *showing* me how to reach this group of people by his own example of care for me. His kindness and humility touched me deeply.

In addition, I watched how Ron interacts in his relaxed manner. Whether he is working at the Nutrition Bar in the reception area, sitting among the drop-ins, or leading a Bible study, he offers a listening ear, a joke, or a warm hug. Or he offers to pray for a brother or sister. In return, Ron receives warm hearty welcomes wherever he goes in the city.

Some call him *Legs* because he wears Tilley shorts year-round and his legs are sturdy and brown like tree trunks, sturdy like the man of God he is. Others call him *Pastor* because of his listening demeanour. "Tell me your story," he often says, drawing alongside some discouraged soul sitting on a dirty staircase. His friends on the street love him for loving them. Often when we are taking a walk, we will hear someone call out, "Ronnie!"

Friendship is the key to their hearts.

Ron recognizes that what marginalized souls want most is to be known by their names, to be treated like a friend, to receive and give a hug, to talk about their broken lives to someone who will listen and care, and to laugh and joke together as well.

Pointing them to Jesus, who loves them, is the ultimate message of hope they need. Though it's the message every heart needs, Ron's philosophy about sharing the gospel is that it's best to *live* it rather than force-feed it. We are the only Bible many people may ever read. But we are also responsible for listening to God's direction about when it's time to clearly explain what Jesus has done for our lost souls.

"For God so loved the world that he gave his only son, that whoever believes in him should not perish but have everlasting life." John 3:16

CHAPTER 14

Turtles on a Log

Our street friends have become very dear to me as well as to Ron, who knows hundreds of them. Besides those I have met through the Drop-In Centre and Bible study, the bus stop across from Our Place has become a hub for surprising interaction.

It was not my intention to make friends with those who congregate at this bus shelter, which I suppose serves as their clubhouse. On Sundays after Subway lunch with Ron and our youngest son, Paul, I headed for the nearest bus stop, which was across from Our Place. Rather than disturb the group, I sat outside the booth on my walker. My goal was to be courteous, keep my head down, and get safely home. But I think God had other plans.

After a few weeks, someone named Liam invited me to squeeze in beside him. Two Metis women scattered to make room for me. I reluctantly accepted the offer and decided to show them a photo of Ron on my cellphone as my security. Once they knew me as the wife of their respected buddy, Ron, this connection became my calling card, my *in* with those who trust few people, for good reason.

Week by week, we began to make conversation. Liam, the warm red-headed Irish man, and I often exchanged a few words and stories. I learned scraps of his background and promised to pray for his health. We joked about the abundance of cabbage at every meal in his Irish childhood. Liam introduced me to two of his drinking mates. Whenever police appeared across the street, the paper-covered bottles disappeared behind the bench.

My new friends began the lovely habit of waving down my bus and escorting me, a tiny woman with a walker, to the entrance in a grand production of care. This must have greatly amused the bus driver and passengers.

When bus #2 arrived, I sometimes ignored it because we were in the middle of a visit. It seemed respectful to hear their full story before I headed back to my cozy condo.

One time, when I was actually eager to catch the first bus home because of the blustery cold, Liam surprised me by telling the others, "Oh, she doesn't take the first bus." And then, he waved the bus to carry on. I hadn't realized that he had noticed.

Mikey, a gentle Metis, was the first person in the shelter I made acquaintance with. Although he was often in various stages of inebriation, we shared many a conversation. One day, he sombrely told me, "I have no soul."

"Oh, Mikey, I assure you, you do have a soul! God has given every human being a soul."

"Tell me," he challenged, "where do thoughts go when we die?"

"Thoughts go with your soul," I said.

"And where does the soul go?"

Here was the nub of the matter. He wanted to hear the truth. I felt compelled to give it straight.

"Our soul has two choices. Either God and Heaven or Satan and Hell."

Apparently, Mikey did not like that answer. He turned his back on me. Our conversation had ended. I did not like that answer either, but we do have a choice.

I asked God for another chance to discuss this eternal topic, but next time I saw Mikey, he was too wasted to talk.

A month later, when I arrived at the shelter, the air was heavy with sadness. Liam explained that they were grieving for a lost brother. A picture of Mikey was taped to the glass partition. He had suffered a pierced organ after he fell into a piece of sharp equipment. They were all raising a bottle to their departed friend. My tears joined theirs.

I pondered our last conversation. Perhaps the stark answer I gave Mikey about Heaven or Hell was exactly what he needed to hear before his life ended. Perhaps he had chosen God and Heaven. I earnestly pray he did.

Meanwhile, I made another new friend in this tightly knit group. It happened on a very stormy Wednesday after our Bible study in the chapel upstairs. As I snugged my scarf around my neck, I considered how to safely navigate the busy crossing to the bus stop while the wind was whipping trees into a frenzied dance.

I spoke to security and asked whether someone could escort me across the street. "Certainly," I was told, "just wait for someone to come back from break." As I waited, I watched a towering figure enter the lobby. He wore a big cowboy hat and cowboy boots.

"Jake!" I smiled. "You're the guardian angel I've been waiting for! Could you possibly take me across the street?" Jake offered me his arm like a gentleman and guided me to the shelter, where he sat with me until my bus arrived.

Another time, when Jake spotted me sitting in the shelter alone, he crossed the street with a boom box bigger than he was, sat next to me, and shared some of his favourite pop songs with me. I can still hear "Hey Jude" in my head. He joked that one of his four sisters had had a boyfriend named Jude. Small talk. But it's a way to share life. Music too can be a great way to bond. We did not need to talk much; we were simply enjoying that lighthearted interlude together.

I learned that Jake is a stone carver who can envision what image a soapstone carries within and then re-create it with special tools. Whales and eagles are some of the wildlife he carved, but I was especially drawn to a tiny turtle. One day, Ron came home with a soft black baggie. Inside was a beautiful green turtle—a gift for me. Since then, Jake has carved a tan turtle for me as well.

On the window shelf by my computer, my friend's two miniature turtles lounge on a *log*, which is really a piece of driftwood from Oak Bay Marina. What inspired the log addition was the sight of many turtles sunning themselves on a log in the pond at Beacon Hill Park this past spring.

It was amusing to watch the Beacon Hill turtles relaxing on a floating tree trunk, until some cheeky pond duck landed on their territory and tipped the log over. Many of the turtles tried to hang on, but a few got dunked in the water. After a few minutes, we watched their claws grab hold and, painstakingly, they climbed back up on their perch. This routine was repeated numerous times a day.

How often our street friends have been dumped into the waters of disappointment, yet they keep on climbing back up, hoping that, someday, they might find the missing pieces to their lives. Maybe, someday, somebody will love them and make it worthwhile for them to get back up. We cannot limit God's presence. Where we go; he goes.

In his excellent book, *God in the Alley*, Greg Paul writes about working among the street-involved of Allan Gardens in Toronto. While he endeavours to *be Jesus* to the marginalized, he expresses the importance of looking for Jesus in those we help as well. Let the broken be Jesus to you and me. When my friends shared their space with me, they are being Jesus to me. When they flagged down my bus and helped me safely board, they were being Jesus to me in my physical vulnerability. In the end, we are all a little bit messed up and need Jesus to show up for us.

CHAPTER 15

Carrying Precious Seed

Feeling numbed by the sad stories of many acquaintances during the COVID-19 pandemic, I could not bear to hear about one more heartbreak. In addition, every newspaper and news report focused on this global outbreak. It overwhelmed my soul, and I began to recognize burnout in me. My blood pressure had climbed too high. I needed to do something differently.

Dr. H suggested that I was taking on the burdens of others and making them my cross. She urged me to take a break and give myself time for myself. Plus, she added a new blood pressure medication to my regimen.

During that time of drawing back, I took solo walks to Beacon Hill Park or the Legislative Fountain area to hear what God had to say to me about carrying other people's crosses. His Word does urge us to carry each other's burdens. So how are we supposed to do that? My pondering and Dr. H's reference to burdens reminded me of a pivotal insight, gleaned many years ago, from my son's perspective.

A Son's Definition

Mark, our first born, gave me deep spiritual insight when he was only six years old. This wisdom still resonates with me today.

Mark sat at the kitchen table playing with his Tonka trucks, while I was pulling a meat loaf from the oven and singing an old chorus about Jesus taking all our burdens away that I had learned in Pioneer Girls.

Mark stopped playing to ask about the song. "Mom, what are burdens?"

"Oh, let me see . . . first give me a minute to set down this hot dish." Inwardly, I was praying for insight as I turned off the oven and turned my attention to those big, earnest brown eyes.

"Well, Mark . . ." I said, stalling for time. "Burdens are useless things we carry around with us . . . like things that worry us."

I was definitely dragging around some worries about my declining health that doctors were ignoring. Singing a song like this helped me to focus on the image of Jesus as my burden bearer.

Mark pondered my response for a while before a light turned on in his young heart.

"Mom, do you mean that burdens are like garbage that a person carries to the curb for the garbage truck? But . . . instead of letting the garbageman take it away, the person picks up the garbage and carries it back into the house."

"Yes, Mark! That is exactly what burdens are like! I never thought of it that way before." I endeavoured to practice his strategy.

A story of meat loaf, a song, and my son's definition of burdens still ring true today!

"He that goeth forth and weepeth, bearing precious seed, shall doubtless come again with rejoicing, bringing his sheaves with him." Psalm 126:6

As a follower of Jesus since age eight, I am acquainted with the tears that come from carrying and watering the precious seed of Jesus's love story for the world to anyone who will listen. Moms and dads understand this. Sunday School teachers and pastors know this. Anyone who cares for the spiritual development of another soul understands.

For decades, this mother and father have been carrying precious seed, planting the love of God in our sons' lives—an imperfect love laced with our own defaults. Yet we continue to water this seed with tears and groans too deep for expression. Their hurts are our hurts; their victories, ours too.

Someday we will rejoice, bringing our harvest with us to the Lord. In fact, if we pay attention, we will see evidence that God has always been at work through our prayers. He is always on his way to bring us victory in the struggle.

A Son's Choice

Our youngest son, Paul, used to say that he could not remember his childhood. This dismayed me. I made a photo album for him and pointed out the many good times of his childhood. No, he could not recall those moments.

After many difficult seasons in his life, he moved to our retirement city of Victoria to spend more time near us. One day, while visiting, he said, "Hey, Mom, I remember the time you told me about Jesus and I said 'yes.'"

"What do you recall about that?" I asked, feeling hope well up within me.

"I was only four, but you gave me a rather long answer to explain Jesus." My son elaborated, "I decided that it made sense to trust in Jesus." Then he left the room, and the conversation ended as abruptly as he had initiated it.

I remembered that precious moment when he said "yes" to Jesus being Lord of his life, but now he remembered it too! I marvelled at the work of the Holy Spirit to remind a son, whose memory was temporarily blocked, about his faith commitment as a child. It is the most important decision a person can make.

After a while, my son returned to add one more detail. "And Mom . . . I still choose Jesus."

Words of life. Our son has no idea how deeply his announcement has thrilled our parental hearts.

As for his memory, he now recalls many wonderful moments in his upbringing that had previously been buried in life's difficulties.

Leaving Home

Three years into our marriage, how we welcomed the arrival of our firstborn, Mark James. Christmas was approaching, and I wanted to do some shopping, so I enlisted Uncle Ken to care for our newborn. As I dressed Mark, nursed him, and waited for my brother's knock at our door, I began to weep. Someday my son would be leaving me. How could I ever bear that! Blame those tears on postpartum blues.

But what was my excuse seventeen years later when Mark left home for the first time? It was unplanned. We gave our blessing as he left on a two-week holiday to Grand Prairie with his high-school buddies.

I promised Mark I would not make his favourite shepherd's pie until he came home. On the day we expected his return, the fragrant casserole was cooling on a rack while I laid down for a nap.

While dozing, I suddenly came to, jumped out of bed, and ran downstairs to Mark's bedroom, thinking I had heard him in my sleep. But he was not there. I opened his closet. All the hangers dangled empty, like skeletons. Mark had come and gone. Back upstairs in the kitchen, I found a brief hand-scrawled note.

> *Mom, me and the guys have decided to rent a house and try life together in Grand Prairie. I came home to get my stuff. Sorry I didn't wake you. I couldn't bear to see the disappointment in your eyes.*

I laid my head on the table and wept. No postpartum blues this time. Just plain old grieving for a son I had carried in my heart all those years.

Mark eventually grew tired of the experiment as his dad had predicted, and he came home for another year to resume classes. A year later, our van was loaded with Mark's belongings, and his dad sat in the idling van outside in the driveway, while Mark came inside to say goodbye to me.

Sadly, Mark and I had been quarrelling the week before his permanent departure from home. We refused to talk to one another about some misunderstanding. Both of us hurt. Maybe it was more about the dread of leaving with as little emotion as possible.

When my son entered the kitchen, I pointed to the care package of food I had ready for him.

Mark stood over me, "Mom, stand up. I want to say goodbye to you."

I didn't want to say goodbye. My heart was breaking again. Who can hear the splintering of a mother's heart each time she says goodbye?

This time was for real. His dad was driving him to the West Coast of Victoria, British Columbia, where he had enrolled in Camosun College's Chef Course. A long way from home in Wetaskiwin, Alberta.

Mark waited, with his arms held out to me. I stood up and received his warm, long hug. "Mom, I *love* you."

I tried not to blubber. Mark knew my heart for him.

Thankfully, our eldest son paved the way for Paul, so when he left home four years later, I had spilled most of my tears, and this time, it was easier. He was our placid child, who preferred to stay close to home.

Paul would only be forty-five minutes away in the city of Edmonton at Mount Carmel Bible College. As a keepsake, I gave him a notebook that he and I had started in Moose Jaw when he was only six. Upon his suggestion, we had kept a record of "A Good Thing That Happened Today." At that time, life had been tentative as I began tri-weekly, life-saving, dialysis treatments, and my youngster thought it worthwhile to focus on happy moments.

Since those days of painful farewells, we all live in British Columbia now and get to see each other more often. Mark comes every Christmas from Vancouver, and Paul lives a few blocks from us in Victoria.

What joy we've had in sharing life with our sons, learning from their perspectives . . . that burdens can be left at the curb for the garbage collector and that there's something good about every day, if you look carefully. That the precious seed we sow reaps a harvest at the right time.

Our sons' journeys have deeply impacted us for our own good. The heartbreak, the triumphs—all are teachers to mature us and bind us to our God, who made our children and knows them best.

CHAPTER 16

Love to Tell the Story

A slender eleven-year-old girl takes a bus to downtown Oakville, Ontario. It's the fifties era. She's looking forward to an afternoon of shopping at Woolworth's on Lakeshore Road at the corner of Dunn Street, where she will spend some of her babysitting earnings.

On her way home, she spots a man in grubby, tattered clothes, staggering in a back alley behind a string of stores. He carries a bottle of booze barely visible from its brown paper covering.

In her head, she can hear her mother warning her to keep walking, but this child's heart is drawn to the pitiful condition of this stranger. Without fear, she turns into the laneway and calls after him.

"Sir, sir." *Her dad had taught her to address all men as gentlemen.*

He turns around, growling. What does she want?

She looks into his red-rimmed eyes and catches a whiff of his alcohol-fuelled breath. In her household, this is an unfamiliar odour. This only serves to increase her urgency.

"Sir, you don't have to live like this," she urges him with clear conviction.

"What does a kid like you know about my life?" he challenges.

"Well, sir, I know that Jesus loves you, and he wants to help you get up and live by faith in him." She explains to him how Jesus stands ready to help every person he created and died for.

Did this infuriate him even more? But wait . . . is he noting that little Miss Salvation's body language telegraphs compassion, not judgment. Maybe his heart melts just a little?

"Thank you, little girl, for stopping to tell me that," he mutters, and she skips to her bus stop, singing a prayer for him.

Whatever prompted this shy girl's response to a broken man in a downtown laneway?

As you probably gathered, that girl was me. Telling others how Jesus can rescue them and how he has cared for me and mine has been among my favourite themes. I'm not sure when or how the seeds were planted in me that prompted this lifelong pursuit. The primary influences came from my household and church.

I recall a new neighbour who was in a heartbreaking domestic situation seeking out my mom for counsel. Mom welcomed her friend with a cup of tea and homemade apple pie, made with apples from our apple trees in the backyard. Mom's pie crust was a bit tough, but for many, the juicy filling spelled comfort.

Mom listened to her story and eventually opened her Bible to John 14 where Jesus tells his disciples not to let their hearts be troubled. Mom shared with her friend from the first verse, *"Let not your heart be troubled. You believe in God, believe also in Me."* Taking in this lesson on compassion, I realized how powerful the Word of God is in giving people comfort and direction.

At my dad's automated car wash, customers often felt comfortable in sharing their private dilemmas with my personable dad. He would roll into an anecdote that pointed to Jesus, and sometimes he offered them a short gospel tract from the display of pamphlets that he kept by the observatory window. Dad prayed regularly for them and followed up to see how they were doing the next time they came around for a car wash.

The songs of my childhood also motivated me. Music played an influential role at the children's clubs, Sunday School, and church services that our family attended. Songs like "This little light of mine, I'm going to let it shine," "Tell me the stories of Jesus I love to hear," and "I will make you fishers of men" made lasting impressions.

But the lyrics that captured my heart most profoundly came from a chorus we learned at Vacation Bible School led by our young Pastor Crawford, who made it his business to learn every child's name.

> *Brightly beams our Father's mercy*
> *From His lighthouse evermore,*
> *But to us He gives the keeping*
> *Of the lights along the shore.*

> *Refrain:*
> *Let the lower lights be burning!*
> *Send a gleam across the wave!*

Some poor fainting, struggling seaman
You may rescue, you may save.

Whenever I heard these words and the plaintive melody written by Philip Paul Bliss, they tugged at my heart. I could not ignore the call. People were struggling, sinking in their tears, and they needed to be rescued.

But as the years passed, I learned that however commendable the goal to *rescue* souls, I could never be the Rescuer. As a mortal with a dark side, I needed rescue too. Even my exemplary pastor could not rescue. Only the perfect, sinless Son of God could do that.

My job was to *point* others to him. That is my privilege and my mandate as his daughter, redeemed by his grace. Being an introvert, who does not want to step on toes and give offence, it is not easy to put myself out there. But to present the gospel message as the Truth does give offence to many, especially in our society that worships at the altar of relativity.

Before Jesus ascended to Heaven, he urged his followers to "Go into all the world and preach the gospel." He did not promise us an easy road, but he did promise to be with us always. Armed with that assurance, my gospel-sharing tradition even spilled over into my dating adventures. Every boy I went out with heard the good news message. My parents encouraged their seven children to be vocal and not to hide their convictions.

Some of the young men I went out with ribbed me about my faith. One cynical date, in particular, named Ron Morgan, challenged my belief in God, saying it was mere wishful thinking, pie in the sky, and a crutch. This dissent got under my skin; he enjoyed watching me defend my position. I guess he liked my feistiness because he continued to ask me out.

Relentlessly, I urged him to consider where his life was headed—he admitted he drank too much—and how different it could be if he gave his life to Christ. After sitting through many church services with my brother, Ken, and then with me, incredibly, Ron began to take me and my God more seriously. And, wonder of wonders, he decided to choose the Jesus way. A year after his decision, I married him, and we've been a united team ever since.

Chain of Command

Though Ron came to Jesus by slow degrees, his faith matured to a place where he became a man of prayer, whom everyone could count on. Every day began in prayer, was lived in prayer, and ended the same. As the manager of a prosperous Mississauga Canadian Tire store with many staff members, Ron understood and respected the chain of command.

He was willing to yield to the voice of God the way a soldier yields to the voice of his commander. This willingness was tested during an ordinary Sunday evening in a prayer service at Calvary Baptist Church in Oakville, Ontario. Out of the blue, Ron whispered that it was time for him to go see his parents.

"Now, Ron?" I asked. It was the middle of the service.

Yes, he was getting his marching orders. NOW.

He drove to his parents' cozy, smoke-filled apartment and solemnly asked them to listen to the challenge he must present to them. He told them that he knew they were good people but, unless they received Jesus as Lord, their entrance into

Heaven was not a given. In John 14:6, Jesus had said only he is the way, the truth, and the life. No man could come to the Father but by him. Ron faithfully offered the message that God had laid on his heart.

Mom and Dad wanted to think on this. They called in our pastor to verify the message, mulled it over, and after a few days, Ron's docile dad made the first move. He wanted to follow Jesus. Then Mae followed suit.

Noticeable changes occurred in each parent. Mae, the dominant partner in the marriage, who had used to curse liberally, began to curtail her language for the sake of Jesus's honour. Arnie, a lifelong alcoholic, suddenly had no further desire for the stuff, and he gave it up in a day. In addition, Arnie testified that one day while smoking alone in his living room, he was thinking about Jesus loving him through his ups and downs. To the Invisible Presence with him, he said, "What must *this* look like to you?" pointing to his cigarette. After a few more puffs, he butted out, never to light another one again. Mae, on the other hand, never gave up her smokes, but Jesus saves by grace, and her faith in him was solid. We were witnesses to another one of God's miracles.

Dad and Mom became members of our Bible-believing church and were baptized to publicly declare their decision. *"Everyone who confesses me before men, I will confess him before my Father in Heaven."* Matthew 10:32

Mom's favourite verse was Psalm 121:1–2, *"I will lift up my eyes unto the hills from whence cometh my help. My help cometh from the LORD who made Heaven and earth,"* and Mae lived that verse the rest of her eighty-two years. Arnie's remaining years, however, were shortened to sixty-eight, due to a diseased liver, yet he stayed on track with his newfound faith. What a thrill for Ron to point his parents to Jesus of the cross, who waits for his followers to join him in Life Eternal, when we pass from this earth.

As a dearly loved adopted child, Ron appreciated the beauty of being able to bring his mom and dad to Jesus, who adopts every person who comes to him in trust.

This success story with his parents opened Ron's heart to consider a new kind of challenge from the Lord, involving a night vision.

CHAPTER 17

Night Vision

Years later in Edmonton, after both sons had left for college, God came to Ron in a night vision. Ron had never experienced such a phenomenon before. He sat up in bed to study the scene before him. He recognized it as a specific site but could not place its whereabouts. In the public square of this vision stood a man holding a gospel tract.

What was he to make of it? The next morning, Ron identified the location at Rice Howard Way in downtown Edmonton. Heading to that site, he asked God to confirm that the vision was a message to act on.

He received his confirmation from our German Baptist pastor who told Ron that he believed God was calling him to be a witness to that core business area.

Ron began to take prayer walks around Rice Howard Way, asking God to prepare the way. Meanwhile, his heart was protesting. "Lord, I can't do this. This is way out of my comfort zone."

He jokes about the doubter in him who sought the services of a lawyer to cover all the legal objections that might arise from embarking on such a mission. The trendy business core would not be a receptive audience to a message that claims to be the truth.

People cushioned by prosperity are the least likely candidates to be aware of their needs or admit they need a Rescuer. Better prospects present themselves in the seedy laneways of the down and out, where people have lost their dreams, jobs, families, and hope. However, Ron knew he needed to go where he was sent.

Ron enlisted me to pray with him. Together we created a foundation called Salt and Light Team—S.A.L.T. for short—with our two sons and two friends as our founding members.

Ron designed an attractive sidewalk sandwich board that stood on a portable stand and posed this question:

IN A WORLD SEEKING SPIRITUALITY,
FULFILLMENT, AND HOPE
WHY JESUS?

He also secured gospel tracts by Nicky Gumbel of the *Alpha* program in Britain, which presented answers to the "why follow Jesus" question.

Was anyone even asking? We were going to learn.

On our first morning out, I sat at a nearby bench, observing and praying, while Ron stood with a tract and his sidewalk sign, inviting people to take a tract. Most walked by, casting a sideways glance and giving Ron a wide berth.

Over time, some showed interest in knowing more about this Jesus. Eventually, a few began to acknowledge Ron by bringing him a coffee; he was becoming a familiar part of the scene. He didn't impede anyone's progress, wasn't in anyone's face. He simply gave a warm greeting and a nod, holding a pamphlet titled *Why Jesus?* which people could help themselves to from the dispenser on our sign.

But others were hostile and determined to remove him and his intrusive question from the area. A businessman questioned Ron's right to stand on public property, so Ron rotated his sites in the Rice Howard Way to minimize the friction and maximize the exposure. I often would spell him off with a fifteen-minute shift, so he could stretch his legs.

Ron's street ministry introduced him to some surprising encounters and friendships.

At one of the bustling sites by a transit centre, Ron noticed a street person, panhandling nearby. The young Metis appeared immaculately groomed and friendly. The two struck up conversations. Ron learned that Chad slept in a downtown garage and washed up daily in a public washroom or at the Y. He shopped at thrift stores, selecting quality clothes with style.

Chad carried his slim, compact frame with a confident swagger.

He was impeccably dressed and groomed with his shiny black hair pulled back in a ponytail, and sported a long, black coat. Every finger was encircled in knuckle rings, and he possessed a winning smile that he flashed at unexpected moments.

Chad, with his many rings and chains, sometimes offered to hold a tract for a while and invite people to take one. They were receptive to his small, but impressive, authoritative figure.

He challenged one well-dressed man with a smile and noted, "Sir, you've started the day with a few drinks, haven't you?"

Takes a drunk to know a drunk. Chad had tried many a program to get off the streets and off the booze, but he missed his people, his comrades on the streets. Flying right can be a lonely life for someone used to being a big fish in his little pond.

He had been a five-star chef in Toronto, but the draw to alcohol got the better of him. He'd gone to rehab a number of times, and while there, he was recognized as a leader and mentor to other hurting people. But he could not resist the street life that gave him a sense of community that he missed while sober. He had a reputation as a tough guy who often instructed his street buddies that no one was to panhandle or harm Ron or me. We privately called him "The Godfather."

We often enjoyed a breakfast sandwich with Chad after our S.A.L.T. watches. He even came to our home one Christmas and cooked a gourmet turkey dinner, a hit with all our guests. Sadly, last we heard, despite many rehab attempts, he could not shake his addiction. After we moved from Alberta, we lost track of him. We consider meeting Chad one of the great gifts of that season of outreach.

Another person who became a dear friend to Ron was Bruce. Ron met this former musician when he had moved his S.A.L.T. location to the City Hall neighbourhood. Bruce lived in a nearby rooming house, and they struck up conversations as fellow believers in Jesus.

Bruce sketched this familiar history of redemption: he had passed out in a drunken daze once too often and begged God to please help him. Without the benefit of AA, he had pulled himself out of his pit through the grace of God. With his prayers, Bruce faithfully supported our ministry. He often came for family dinners at our home, and he and Ron became dear friends.

Bruce's story reminds me of the heartbreaking song called "Help Me," written by Larry Gatlin and made famous by Elvis Presley. It tells the story of a world-weary and tired man who pleads with God to give him strength to walk one more mile.

The last time we saw Bruce, it was to say goodbye because we were going to Victoria for our winter retreat. Within a few days of our departure, we had a call from the Edmonton police. Bruce, who was diabetic, had collapsed on his apartment floor and died alone. And yet not alone. We are trusting that Jesus or one of his angels was there with him to usher him Home.

When Bruce died, there was no family member to claim his body, so Ron returned to Edmonton to clean out his apartment, and to arrange for his burial with a marker to honour the life Bruce had lived.

CHAPTER 18

Angels Among Us

Speaking of angels, before every S.A.L.T. encounter, we always prayed together for Ron to be surrounded with angels. We could not see them, but we knew we needed to enlist all Heaven's resources in this spiritual endeavour that Satan resists.

Two mornings a week, in all seasons, Ron stood in Edmonton's downtown core. Many winter mornings, the snow swirled fiercely around Ron, this lone figure standing on a street corner for the name of Jesus, like the prayer warrior God meant him to be, while people hurried by to their offices and on shopping errands.

One particular morning, as people shuffled by, an approaching woman shouted to Ron and pointed at something behind him. He looked around. What was she so upset about? Ron leaned closer, asking her to explain what she meant.

She stepped away from him. "No! Don't come closer!" She pointed again. "Angels, look at all the angels!" she said, indicating with her hand that they were all around Ron. This woman saw the angels that God sent to guard Ron at his faithful post. Her declaration sent a thrill down Ron's spine.

CHAPTER 19

Howling at the Moon

Despite these recent rewarding years in Victoria, I have experienced moments of searing doubt. How odd after all these years. But doubts test our resolve to stay with it and trust when we cannot feel our faith anymore.

In Mother Teresa's private journals, she revealed that she experienced intense doubts of God's love and reality, and yet, she carried on as though she believed, so as not to discourage others from believing. This revelation heartened me. To think that such a saint also faced temptations and survived them.

My *Streams in the Desert* classic devotional began the reading for May 20 with the suggestion that suffering can be a gift for our soul, but forgotten after the crisis has passed.

Yes, I know about how easy it is to forget the lessons. They can be elusive. When the trial has lifted, I cannot remember. *What are the gifts in suffering?* Did I ever learn them sufficiently for them to kick in the next time a trial rises up? Honestly, my main goal through episodes of pain is to get them over with as quickly as possible. Never mind the lessons!

The *Streams* writer offered this insight: that if one opens their heart to pain and suffering, it will accomplish more than resistance will. *How does a person open his heart to suffering? And why take that risk?* I've read similar advice in other devotional pages, and it sounds lofty and doable on a good day. But when I'm immobilized with arthritic pain, the words fall on a cold heart.

Ron's seventieth birthday had been uneventful aside from celebrating with cake and ice cream. I suppose it was the sugary icing that set me up.

Tiny shards of uric acid crystals plowed through the blood vessels of my left hand, causing my entire arm to ache incessantly with gout.

Ice packs gave some relief. Surrendering to the pain and falling asleep gave some relief. But by 2:00 a.m., I woke to even more intensive and sustained pain.

I sat in our brown leather chair by an open window where a lovely breeze wafted over me on that warm August night. I tried to find a quiet place in me, so I could endure. But I could not find it.

The only thing that registered was intense anger at God. Why so angry with God? Because he was allowing me another test, and I was failing miserably. Nighttimes are usually the worst, when the "wolves of Hell" unleash their attacks on broken bodies and minds.

Restless with escalating pain and rage, I paced our small apartment. Back and forth. Through the kitchen and into the living room. Beside myself. Pausing at our big picture window, which faces west, I stood to view the full moon, radiating its rays across the waves of Juan de Fuca Strait.

This scene has always thrilled my soul. But not this night. The beauty seemed to mock me. *GOD* seemed to mock me.

My misery combusted into action. I shook my fist at the full moon and at the God who made it. Before I could stop myself, my mouth was spewing a verbal stream against my Creator.

"I hate you, God! I hate you! I hate you, Jesus! I hate you!"

Words I have never spoken before. Horrible, unforgivable words. I imagined God as a heartless overlord who was enjoying my misery, sticking me with pins to curse my life.

Then I returned to bed feeling that Hell could be my only destiny. Curiously, I slept like a baby.

In the morning when Ron asked me how I was doing, I said, "I think I am going to Hell." Then, I described what I had done.

Sitting on the edge of my bed, my husband tenderly held my hand. "Hon, God knows your heart. He knows that you want to please him and trust him . . . but the trials go on and on."

I wept.

Yes, God knows my heart. He understands everything about me. Every hateful part of me. Every earnest intention. Every hurtful thought. Every tender prayer. Every vengeful emotion. Every kind gesture. Every miserable murmur and every beautiful thing. I am reminded of Romans 5:8, *"For while we were yet sinners, Christ died for us."*

Lord, how could you endure such hateful abuse by your own creatures, so many dreadful accusations against you—like the insults I hurled at you last night? I am not capable of loving your way. It is beyond my ability and often not even my desire. It seems unattainable.

As I reflected on this painful memory, I realized that many are tormented by their failure to do better. In Romans 7, the apostle, Paul, agonized that the things he wanted to do, he couldn't, and the things he should not do, he did. As he states in verses 21 and 24, *"Although I want to do good, evil is right there with me. What a wretched man I am! Who will rescue me from this body that is subject to death?"*

Paul's concluding statement, in Romans 7:25, was one of rescue and relief. *"Thanks be to God who delivers me, through Jesus Christ our Lord!"*

That night of desperation drove me to test that God is more gracious than I knew. I expected condemnation; he gave me reassurance. He already knows my inner thoughts and wants me to give them all to him.

In its place, God is doing his redeeming work in me. A work of repentance and reliance, eventually creating a clearer image of his beauty in the way I respond when trouble rises again.

George Matheson, a blind Scottish pastor, wrote these timeless lyrics at a time of heartrending loss, published in 1882.

> *"O Joy that seekest me through pain,*
> *I cannot close my heart to thee;*
> *I trace the rainbow through the rain,*
> *And feel the promise is not vain,*
> *That morn shall tearless be."*

Reflections on Coping

Since that explosive night lesson, kidney disease with its complications has given me many more opportunities to handle my painful episodes with more trust in his forgiving, understanding love. He who endured a humiliating death for mankind understands suffering more than anyone. He can use our suffering to create something better in us. A better way to adapt to our circumstances.

Music has played a key role in relieving the intensity of my pain. The Internet offers an abundance of soothing instrumental music for a frantic spirit. Music with water or birdsong in the background can quiet the raging throb in our bodies and souls. Similarly, listening to soothing meditation apps like "Abide" before bedtime can quiet the overwrought mind.

Reminding ourselves of God's promises in scripture can fix our minds on his truths. Promises such as Hebrews 13:5, "*He has said, I will never leave you nor forsake you,*" or 1 Peter 5:7, "*Casting all your cares upon him because he cares for you*" can help refocus our minds on the things that bring life.

Lastly, nurturing a grateful attitude is paying off. Throughout each day, God draws my attention to something lovely that happened to me, some sign of his love in my circumstance. The way sunshine falls across the room, the beauty of a flower, or the gift of a quiet space within me where the Father speaks to me.

My habit of keeping a prayer journal has evolved into a notebook of thanksgiving for little blessings. I'm learning the power in thanking God that he is working all things for good to those who love him. Rather than prayers of desperation, my

86

prayers are turning into thanksgiving for what God is about to do to meet the need.

Better to bless than curse. Blessing our way through trying circumstances and difficult people releases Heaven's resources. I am slowly learning to, as Psalm 103:1 admonishes, *"Bless the Lord, oh my soul, and all that is within me, bless his holy name."*

CHAPTER 20

Our Love Story

The thing about setbacks is that when the better times come, they seem far sweeter. Nothing is taken for granted.

Take our love story. Amazingly, the heart of our marriage is still beating strong. Not to say, there are no blips or murmurs, but we are standing the test of time.

We are still committed to a weekly date with each other. Late Saturday mornings after Ron has served his shift at Our Place, he takes me on a leisurely walk through picturesque James Bay to the Juan de Fuca Strait on Dallas Road. Ron walks alongside me while I ride my motorized scooter.

We find a secluded bench on a bluff protected by the sea wall where we can watch the surf roll onto the shore below. Here and there, we spot a sailboat or motorboat plying the waters. Colourful kites in the distance float across the sky. And walkers pass our bench with cases of beverage as they head down to the beach.

Ron places an amplifier between us and chooses Fifties on Five from his cellphone; we listen to SiriusXM Radio play our favourite oldies, like "Love Letters in the Sand," and others, on the Pat Boone hour. We share a treat and smile contentedly. This is the life.

Some walkers smile as they pass by and wave. One lady gaily calls to us from the sidewalk above us, saying, "Nothing like rock and roll . . . and Oreos." She gives our choice a thumbs-up.

I wonder if people can tell we have been together for fifty-one years. Not an easy fifty-one years, but who gets an easy life?

Ron and I reminisce about our fiftieth celebration a year before. We wanted to make it extra special, but, given my health, it did not seem feasible to take a cruise or a train trip. So, we opted for simple, but elegant. We caught a ferry to Vancouver across the strait and took the SkyTrain to our luxury condo booking in pretty Olympic Village. Usually we opt for a cheap, functional motel in Mount Pleasant, but fifty years requires some splurging.

We packed our raincoats because Vancouver is green year-round for good reason. That first week of May 2019 could not have been more perfect. Not one moment of rain. Only balmy, sunny days.

Our elegant condo overlooked False Creek along which we followed lovely walkways, leading to a core of upscale eating places and the humble McDonald's franchise where we enjoyed a SKOR McFlurry.

We met our older son, Mark, for lunch at City Centre Mall, and were eager to tell him about our amazing digs and our wonderful Airbnb host, David, who made us feel extremely welcome.

We told Mark, who works in the Vancouver film industry, about the luxury of a big screen television and watching a different box office movie every night. We chose *I Saw the Light*, a Hank Williams story with great country tunes like "Hey, Good Lookin'" and "I'm So Lonesome I Could Cry."

Best of all we got to watch the movie, *The Shack*, on which our son had worked as set decorator. We learned that Mark had the privilege to build Jesus's Carpenter Shop. It had been a surreal experience for him and for us to witness our son's creativity on film.

Twice, Ron and I visited Granville Island Market where we enjoyed a window view of the courtyard and English Bay and watched the seagulls float above visitors and try to nab their succulent fish fillets. This time, though, the gulls were monitored by a raptor with his trainer—the raptor giving those pests the evil eye. It was a very effective strategy to give guests peace of mind, and yet it provided a fascinating display of this beautiful creature.

On Friday, our official anniversary, we headed once more to the Market and sat at a window seat. I had planned a unique gift for our occasion and decided the best time to deliver it was shortly after we settled into our sunny, private corner.

To be clear, I'm not very creative when it comes to gifts, so we usually agree not to exchange gifts. Besides, we both have more than enough. But this inspiration came to me in an oblique way.

Earlier that March, my lovely friend, Marina, and I had both been feeling rather blue with the grey days, so she suggested we each write a poem with the same theme to cheer each other on.

"What theme, Marina?"

"You choose, Liz."

I chose the theme of Park Benches since we have met at the park for some of our outings.

"And, Liz, the poem deadline is the last day of March."

I panicked. "But I haven't written a poem in decades!" I protested.

That was the challenge.

I decided that the best place to find inspiration was to begin my project by sitting on a park bench where I could think and take notes. Every few days, I headed to the same bench at Beacon Hill with my red notebook and pen. Bit by bit a story began to unfold.

In my mind, I envisioned all the park benches that Ron and I have visited in our long history together. After numerous edits, I finished my epic poem and even sprinkled photos of those locations between the stanzas. To create a pleasing presentation, I arranged to have Staples print my pages on good quality paper that was bound in a sunny yellow cover—Ron's favourite colour.

When the end of the month arrived, I announced to my friend that the poem was completed, but I could not show it to her until I had given it to Ron in May. We agreed to postpone our poetry-sharing session until after my getaway with Ron. But I was grateful that Marina's spontaneity had produced this wonderful inspiration.

The moment had arrived. I held my breath. What if Ron didn't like it? Another dear friend, who is a cheerleader for many, had urged me to think more positively. Pamela had encouraged me, saying, "Liz! Ron will *love* it! Because it's from your heart!"

Yes, that was the right attitude to lead with. I handed the yellow folder to my sweetheart. "A gift for us, my Love," I smiled.

"What's this?" Ron asked in his business-as-usual fashion.

"Just open it and see."

He opened it and noted that it had many pages. "Oh, it's long!"

Talk about a cold-water response. I needed to give my husband time to transition into a more receptive mode. The iconic fifties television detective, Sgt. Joe Friday, from *Dragnet*, used to say, "Just the facts, ma'am, just the facts." That definitely describes my husband's line of thinking.

I didn't have to wait long for his second response. As he began to read the opening page, I could sense the mood changing. The words had found his heart, and he was undone. He could not speak. His eyes and throat were full. He turned each page, lingered, and then after the last page, he closed the book and sat very still.

This is our love story, a story of heartbreak and of victory. Victory in Jesus who put us together to last forever, to endure the hardships, because he was walking every step with us. *"A strand of three cannot be easily broken."* Ecclesiastes 4:12

Once Upon a Bench

For Ronnie, my True Love of over fifty years
May 10, 2019
By Elizabeth Morgan

A mystery unfolds . . .
On a bench by the lake,
Not any bench—
But one remembered place.

While watching her talk
The young man makes a choice,
His heart will change its course
A decision not made lightly.

Her God is not yet his
But he will try,
To connect the dots
That lead to Heaven.

For better for worse,
Vows said sincerely,
Entrusting their union to God—
Only He can keep promises safe.

When sickness and suffering
Stole through their garden,
Nipping the bloom
From his fair bride.

He became her wounded warrior
Fighting on bended knees for her,

Searching the horizon for a sunny side—
Believing God hears every cry.

But when the trials kept rolling in,
Like a restless foaming surf,
She sometimes wondered why,
Faith and love were not swept away?

An answer came one shimmering day
While sauntering through a park,
He beckoned her to a bench by the lake—
One from their youthful years.

This is the place, he whispered gently,
When I knew that choosing you
Meant choosing Jesus too,
My heart was in, I chose you both.

Perhaps, he added, a selfish choice
But God, it seems, has honoured it,
You see, He blessed us, Bride of my youth,
With a precious three-strand bond.

For fifty years these True Sweethearts
Have shared a weathered bench,
Beside a lake, beside a sea
Shoulders touching, hearts at ease.

Watching ships and sailing vessels,
While nodding hi to passersby,
Content to savour every crumb
Of Love's sweet history.

CHAPTER 21

Why I Still Believe

After reading my first book, a friend and spiritual mentor, Roger, urged me to write a paper on a topic close to his heart. "What I want to know," he said, "is why do you still believe in God?"

Hmmm, *why do I still believe?* What a profound question. So, I began a notebook with this title. After all these years of physical setbacks, what keeps me walking down that road with God?

I've been disappointed in myself because the reasons have not rolled out of my pen in a steady stream as I thought they ought. They've consisted of halting sporadic jots.

When one is younger, it is easier to rise above overwhelming circumstances, but as the body wears down, one's morale can falter too. During this COVID-19 time period of isolation for all, I've been challenged by its subtle effect on own my sense of well-being. I did not expect such an outcome.

I question the best way to spend even more downtime at home. Because of chronic illness and fatigue, this has been my lot for years, but, at least, there were breaks in the solitude when I could meet a friend for lunch or gather with fellow believers at church to celebrate our Lord and each other.

At the beginning of this social distancing, I welcomed my solitary walks to the nearest park, taking my lunch and a good book. I still do. Yet this can become a lonely routine if there is no way to share the experience and observations with another person. Therefore, I've resumed journalling to mine the gold in these unusual times.

At first, I didn't miss the busyness and interaction at Our Place and church because I was growing deeply weary of it all. Sometimes, I just lose interest in life's routines. But this world crisis has turned my thinking upside down, and that is not a bad thing. This hypervigilance of healthy distancing may be overkill, but it can work in one's favour.

Introspection is a valuable exercise if it leads to recognition of where we're at and where we really want to head. Sometimes, we discover that we have gotten off the main road and need to retrace our steps.

I'm discovering that I still carry a backpack of negative habits that need to be replaced with a healthier mindset. I have passed through seasons when I have been angry with my lot in life. Angry when I see others breezing through life—or so it seems—without having to factor in the challenges of chronic illness. Recently, when I confessed this inner rage to my long-suffering husband and to a trustworthy friend, both listened with a posture of compassion. It was a relief to speak my pain and be heard. In that act, I felt the load lift from my self-sorry heart.

Fact is, there will always be someone better off than us, and someone worse off than us as well. Life is unequal.

In the end, I realize my quarrel is with God who is sovereign over this universe and allows evil and sickness to coexist with the beauty he created.

We have been given the gift of free will, but it's an experiment that we humans have miserably abused. Didn't God know we would mess it up for him and for each other? Yes, he did. So why did he take that chance?

After wrestling through these existential issues, I believe God does not want you and me to serve him like automated robots without the power to choose him out of love and honour. A soul that's free to choose evil is a soul that's free to choose good as well.

Through my weekly bouts with one chronic condition after another, I am compelled to reconcile my doubts with my faith in God that flows like a refreshing spring deep within my soul. It has been a very difficult journey, but it is the one ordained for me and mine by an all-wise Creator and Lover of our souls.

I am finding that God stands ready to respond to every cry of my heart when I am honest with myself and with him. The most welcome sight for God is a wandering child who comes running home to him, knowing she needs his help and can't carry on without him. Larry Gatlin's song "Help Me" is a cry that humbles the self-sufficient heart and opens the floods of Heaven's resources.

So, let me name the reasons that I still believe in God. More than ever before . . .

I suppose a major benefit is that suffering and being able to communicate it allows me a platform for presenting a believable gospel that has been proven by the stress tests of time. My courageous friend, Michelle, poses this same reason as her consolation for multiple facial reconstruction surgeries due to cancer's angry assaults. For her, the greatest thrill is to draw alongside a hurting brother or sister and walk with them because she is well-acquainted with the faithfulness of God in her own broken life.

I still believe in God because he has been my Shepherd through every season of drought and abundance. He has led me to still waters and continues to restore my dry, bitter soul by urging me to bless and curse not. Bless everything in sight because God is near and good.

Jesus is the Living Word on whom I can count. Some may say the Bible is a self-help book and a crutch for those who can't hack life. But my reality check is this: I can't hack life on my own strength! I need Jesus, the Word who came in flesh—God With Us—to redeem you and me from ourselves. Michael W. Smith, who wrote the beautiful lyrics to "Ancient Words," invites us to meditate on God's holy words, preserved for all generations, enabling us to walk in this world of troubles.

The ancient words of the Bible lead me to believe though I'll never understand most of its content. I don't need to understand, but I can trust the Spirit of God who moved men to write each book within the Book.

When Jesus asked his disciples if they wanted to leave him as many others had, Simon Peter answered him, "LORD, to whom shall we go? You have the words of eternal life."

In Psalm 73, the writer was grieving the inequality of life and embittered by callous mankind who grows fat on

self-indulgence and mocks God. Eventually he boiled down
the point of faith to this declaration:

> [25] *Whom have I in Heaven but you?*
> *And there is nothing on earth that I desire*
> *besides you.*
> [26] *My flesh and my heart may fail,*
> *but God is the strength of my heart and my*
> *portion forever.*

During those cynical seasons when I can think of no other
reason to still follow Jesus, The Psalmist's and Peter's answer
echoes in my heart. There is no one else worthy to trust in.
Only God, with his perfect, yet bruised, heart can walk with
me in the darkest places.

On our living room wall hangs a comforting scene of three
children trudging home in the snow. When they reach their
farmhouse, dusk is falling, but they are greeted by their barking
dog and a set of lights that glow from the kitchen window.

For me, this picture reflects my mother who was always
waiting to welcome her seven children home. Johnny Cash
sang about his mother, who at the end of each day would ask,
"Are all the children in?"

I can hear God asking that same question. He who made us
and has invested his life in us, who created this beautiful world
for us, does he not care that all his children are safely Home?
God is the Light in the window that waits for you and me.

When I have stood at the bedside of many a dying friend,
I've been led to say what I can envision—that Jesus is standing
near, holding out his hand. "Put your hand in his hand; he
knows the way Home," I say to the Buddhist friend who fears
she will not reach Nirvana, to the mother of a friend who has

ignored God much of her life, to the lovely believing woman who has been wronged by her nearest and dearest. When they receive the simple words, an expression of peace washes over each tense face, and they nod in understanding.

But we don't need to wait until our deathbeds to put our hands in his. Now is the best time. Now is the time to let go of all that we hold onto and let God be the Light on our walk in this life. He will enable us to overcome our difficulties and trust him for one more mile.

The End.

Printed in Canada